Controversial Ideologies in Power: Assessing the Impact on Democracy

Copyright Page

TITLE: Controversial Ideologies in Power: Assessing the Impact on Democracy

1ST Edition

Copyright @ 2023

ISBN: 9798223690740

Table of Contents

Controversial Ideologies in Power: Assessing the Impact on Democracy

By Roberto Miguel Rodriguez

Chapter 1: When Democracy Does Not Work: Assessing the Impact on Democracy

Palestinians Elected Hamas

Introduction:

The election of Hamas, a controversial and radical political movement, by the Palestinian people has raised significant concerns and sparked debates about the compatibility of democracy with the rise of extremist ideologies. This subchapter seeks to analyze and assess the impact of Palestinians electing Hamas as their governing party, shedding light on the complex interplay between democracy, radical political movements, and their consequences on both domestic and international levels.

Understanding the Context:

In order to comprehend the reasons behind the election of Hamas, it is crucial to consider the socio-economic factors and political dynamics that shaped Palestinian society. Factors such as poverty, unemployment, and political disillusionment played a significant role in the rise of Hamas, as Palestinians sought an alternative to the perceived corruption and inefficiency of the existing political parties.

The Role of Political Parties in the Democratic Process:

The election of Hamas underscores the importance of political parties in the democratic process. It highlights the need for diverse and inclusive party systems that address the needs and aspirations of the entire electorate. This subchapter will delve into the specific characteristics of Hamas as a political party and its impact on the democratic process in Palestine.

Assessing the Consequences of Electing Leaders with Controversial Ideologies:

The election of Hamas had far-reaching consequences, not only for Palestinians but also for the broader region. This subchapter will explore the domestic and international ramifications of electing leaders with controversial ideologies, including the impact on peace negotiations, regional stability, and the legitimacy of the Palestinian leadership.

Analyzing the Relationship between Democracy and Radical Political Movements:

The rise of Hamas poses important questions about the relationship between democracy and radical political movements. Scholars will examine whether democracies provide fertile ground for such movements to emerge and thrive or if these movements exploit democratic processes to gain power before undermining democratic principles.

Evaluating the Efficacy of Democratic Systems in Managing Political Transitions:

The election of Hamas raises questions about the efficacy of democratic systems in managing political transitions and ensuring stability. This subchapter will assess the challenges faced by democracies in maintaining stability during times of political polarization and the potential impact on democratic institutions and values.

Conclusion:

The election of Hamas by the Palestinian people serves as a case study to understand the complexities of democracy, the rise of radical political movements, and the challenges they pose to stability and legitimacy. By analyzing the specific context of Palestinians electing Hamas, scholars can gain insights into the broader issues of voter behavior, the impact of socio-economic factors, foreign interference, and the long-term effects of electing leaders with controversial ideologies. Ultimately, this subchapter aims to contribute to a comprehensive understanding of the challenges faced by democracies worldwide and the potential solutions to address them.

Nicaraguans Elected Ortega

In the realm of controversial ideologies in power, the case of Nicaraguans electing Daniel Ortega stands out as a significant and thought-provoking example. This subchapter delves into the complexities surrounding Ortega's rise to power and the subsequent impact on democracy in Nicaragua. Addressing a scholarly audience, it aims to provide a comprehensive analysis of the factors, consequences, and challenges associated with electing leaders with controversial ideologies.

Ortega's ascension to presidency in Nicaragua has been marked by a multitude of debates and controversies. As scholars, it is crucial to examine the underlying causes that led to his electoral success. One aspect to explore is the role of political parties in the democratic process. Understanding the dynamics between Ortega's Sandinista National Liberation Front (FSLN) and other political parties sheds light on the complex interplay of ideologies and voter behavior.

Moreover, socioeconomic factors play a significant role in electoral outcomes. By analyzing the impact of these factors on Nicaraguan elections, scholars can gain insights into the motivations and concerns of the electorate. This analysis becomes particularly relevant when considering the rise of populist leaders within democratic societies, as Ortega's populist appeal played a pivotal role in his electoral success.

Assessing the consequences of electing leaders with controversial ideologies is of utmost importance. By studying Ortega's presidency, scholars can evaluate the long-term effects of leaders with socialist or leftist agendas on democratic systems. This examination also necessitates an exploration of the challenges faced by democracies in maintaining stability during times of political polarization, as witnessed in Nicaragua.

Foreign interference in democratic elections has become a prevalent concern globally. Investigating the role of external actors in Nicaragua's electoral processes provides a valuable perspective on the complexities surrounding democratic elections and their vulnerabilities.

Ultimately, this subchapter aims to contribute to the broader discussions surrounding democracy and radical political movements. By evaluating the efficacy of democratic systems in managing political transitions and studying the factors influencing voter behavior, scholars can gain a deeper understanding of the intricacies and challenges inherent in democratic processes.

In conclusion, the election of Daniel Ortega in Nicaragua presents an intriguing case study for scholars seeking to assess the impact of controversial ideologies on democracy. By examining the role of political parties, socioeconomic factors, and populist appeals, as well as analyzing the consequences and challenges associated with electing leaders with controversial ideologies, a more nuanced understanding of Nicaragua's democratic journey can be achieved. This subchapter seeks to contribute to the ongoing dialogue on democracy's ability to navigate ideological complexities and maintain stability in times of political polarization.

Chileans Elected Allende

In the history of democracy, few elections have been as impactful and controversial as the one that took place in Chile in 1970. It was a moment that exemplified the power of democratic processes, but also revealed the potential risks and challenges that come with electing leaders with controversial ideologies. The election of Salvador Allende, a self-proclaimed socialist, as the President of Chile brought forth a series of political and socioeconomic transformations that still reverberate today.

The election of Allende was a pivotal moment for Chilean democracy. It marked the first time a Marxist candidate had been democratically elected as the head of state in a Western country. Allende's victory represented a significant shift in the political landscape, as it challenged the traditional power structures and economic interests that had long dominated Chilean society. His platform promised radical reforms aimed at reducing inequality, nationalizing industries, and empowering the working class.

However, Allende's presidency was not without controversy. His policies and ideology clashed with the interests of powerful domestic and international actors, leading to a series of conflicts and tensions that eventually culminated in a military coup in 1973. The aftermath of the coup brought about a dark period in Chilean history, characterized by human rights abuses, repression, and the establishment of a military dictatorship under General Augusto Pinochet.

The election of Allende raises important questions about the relationship between democracy and radical political movements. It forces us to consider the limits and challenges of democratic systems when confronted with leaders who propose drastic and controversial changes. It also highlights the role of political parties in the democratic process, as they play a crucial role in shaping public opinion, mobilizing voters, and mediating between different ideological positions.

Moreover, Allende's election invites us to reflect on the impact of socioeconomic factors on electoral outcomes. The popularity of his socialist agenda can be understood within the context of widespread social inequality and economic disparities in Chile at the time. It underscores the potential influence of socioeconomic grievances on voter behavior and the importance of addressing these issues in order to maintain stable and inclusive democracies.

The case of Chile also underscores the long-term effects of electing leaders with socialist or leftist agendas. It raises the question of whether these leaders can effectively manage political transitions and navigate the complexities of governing in a democratic society. It also invites us to consider the challenges faced by democracies in maintaining stability during times of political polarization, as the election of Allende deepened divisions within Chilean society and ultimately led to a breakdown in democratic institutions.

In conclusion, the election of Allende in Chile was a watershed moment in the history of democracy. It revealed both the potential of democratic processes to bring about radical change and the risks and challenges associated with electing leaders with controversial ideologies. Understanding the consequences of such elections is crucial for scholars and those interested in assessing the impact of controversial ideologies on democracy. By studying this case, we can gain valuable insights into the factors influencing voter behavior, the role of political parties, and the challenges faced by democracies in managing political transitions.

Americans Elected Carter and Biden

The election of Jimmy Carter and Joe Biden as presidents of the United States stands out as significant occurrences in American history. Both leaders were elected at different times, facing unique challenges and controversies. This subchapter delves into the reasons behind the election of Carter and Biden, examining the impact of their controversial ideologies on American democracy.

Jimmy Carter, the 39th President of the United States, was elected in 1976, during a time of political and economic turmoil. Carter, a Democrat, campaigned on a platform of government transparency, human rights, and addressing the energy crisis. His election was seen as a response to the Watergate scandal and a desire for change after the Vietnam War. Scholars have analyzed the factors that led to Carter's victory, including his appeal as an outsider and a moralist, as well as his emphasis on human rights.

Joe Biden, the 46th President of the United States, was elected in 2020, amidst a deeply divided nation and a global pandemic. Biden, also a Democrat, campaigned on a platform of unity, reversing Trump-era policies, and tackling the COVID-19 crisis. His election was seen as a rejection of the previous administration's divisive rhetoric and policies. Scholars have examined the impact of Biden's experience and perceived empathy, as well as his ability to build a broad coalition, on his electoral success.

The election of both Carter and Biden raises important questions about the role of political parties in the democratic process. How do party platforms and ideologies shape voter behavior? What role do party endorsements and campaign strategies play in electoral outcomes? These questions are essential to understand the dynamics of American democracy and the choices made by voters.

Furthermore, the election of Carter and Biden highlights the impact of socioeconomic factors on electoral outcomes. How do economic conditions, income inequality, and unemployment rates influence voter decisions? Do voters prioritize social issues or economic policies when casting their ballots? Scholars have explored these questions to gain insights into the complex relationship between socioeconomic factors and electoral outcomes.

In conclusion, the elections of Jimmy Carter and Joe Biden as presidents of the United States represent significant moments in American democracy. Examining the reasons behind their victories and the impact of their controversial ideologies provides valuable insights into the functioning of democratic systems. This subchapter contributes to the larger discussion on controversial ideologies in power and their impact on democracy.

Chapter 2: The Role of Political Parties in the Democratic Process

The Function of Political Parties

In any democratic society, political parties play a crucial role in the functioning of the political system. They serve as the primary vehicles for the expression of political ideas, the mobilization of citizens, and the translation of public opinion into government policies. This subchapter aims to delve into the multifaceted function of political parties in the democratic process, addressing the concerns and interests of scholars and individuals interested in understanding the dynamics of political power.

Political parties serve as the foundation of democratic governance by providing citizens with a variety of choices and representing diverse ideologies and interests. They act as intermediaries between the government and the people, acting as a link that bridges the gap between citizens and policymakers. By offering distinct policy platforms and competing for the support of voters, parties ensure that society's concerns and preferences are reflected in the decision-making process.

Moreover, political parties play a crucial role in fostering political stability and accountability. They serve as a mechanism for organizing political power, allowing for the peaceful transfer of power through electoral processes. By establishing clear lines of responsibility and accountability, parties help prevent the concentration of power in the hands of a single individual or group, thereby safeguarding democratic principles.

The rise of populist leaders in democratic societies has brought the role of political parties into sharper focus. Populist movements often challenge established party systems, relying on charismatic leaders and simplistic messages to mobilize support. It is essential for scholars and political observers to analyze the consequences of electing leaders with controversial ideologies and the impact this has on the democratic process.

Furthermore, the efficacy of democratic systems in managing political transitions is a critical area of study. Democratic transitions can be delicate processes, especially in times of political polarization. Understanding the challenges faced by democracies in maintaining stability during such periods is crucial for scholars and policymakers to ensure the long-term sustainability of democratic governance.

In conclusion, the function of political parties in a democratic society is multifaceted and essential. They serve as the vehicles for expressing political ideas, mobilizing citizens, and translating public opinion into government policies. By understanding their role and analyzing their impact, scholars can contribute to a deeper comprehension of the intricacies of democratic governance and the challenges it faces.

Political Party Systems in Democracies

Introduction

In any democratic society, political parties play a crucial role in shaping the political landscape and influencing the direction of governance. This subchapter aims to provide a comprehensive analysis of political party systems in democracies, exploring their impact on electoral outcomes, the democratic process, and the challenges they face in maintaining stability during times of political polarization. It also delves into the consequences of electing leaders with controversial ideologies, particularly those with socialist or leftist agendas.

The Role of Political Parties in the Democratic Process

Political parties are the main vehicles through which citizens participate in the democratic process. They serve as a platform for political mobilization, representation, and policy formulation. By organizing and articulating citizens' interests and ideologies, political parties provide clarity and choice to voters during elections. Scholars have long debated the extent to which political parties truly represent the interests of the people, or if they are merely vehicles for vested interests and power consolidation.

The Impact of Socioeconomic Factors on Electoral Outcomes

Socioeconomic factors, such as income inequality, education levels, and unemployment rates, significantly influence electoral outcomes. Voters often base their choices on how parties and their leaders address these issues. This subchapter examines the relationship between socioeconomic factors and electoral outcomes, highlighting the ways in which parties strategically appeal to voters' concerns and aspirations.

The Rise of Populist Leaders in Democratic Societies

Populist leaders have gained traction in recent years, challenging the established political order in democratic societies. This subchapter explores the reasons behind the rise of populist leaders, their appeal to certain segments of society, and the implications for democratic governance. It also analyzes the strategies employed by populist leaders to gain and consolidate power.

Assessing the Consequences of Electing Leaders with Controversial Ideologies

Democracies occasionally elect leaders with controversial ideologies, which can have far-reaching consequences for social, economic, and political systems. This subchapter evaluates the impact of such leaders on democratic institutions, civil liberties, and political stability. It delves into case studies, including the elections of Hamas in Palestine, Ortega in Nicaragua, Allende in Chile, Carter and Biden in the United States, and explores the lessons learned from these experiences.

Analyzing the Relationship between Democracy and Radical Political Movements

Democracy often faces challenges from radical political movements that seek to undermine its core principles. This subchapter analyzes the relationship between democracy and radicalism, examining the factors that contribute to the emergence and growth of such movements. It also explores the strategies employed by democracies to counteract radicalism and maintain stability.

Conclusion

Political party systems in democracies are complex and multifaceted. They shape electoral outcomes, influence policy formulation, and determine the overall direction of governance. However, they are not immune to challenges, such as the rise of populist leaders, foreign interference, and maintaining stability during times of political polarization. Understanding the intricacies of political party systems is crucial for scholars and policymakers alike, as it helps identify the strengths and weaknesses of democratic systems and fosters informed discussions on how to improve democratic governance.

The Influence of Political Parties on Electoral Outcomes

Introduction:

In the realm of democracy, political parties play a crucial role in shaping electoral outcomes. Their ideologies, policies, and strategies can significantly impact the choices made by voters, resulting in diverse electoral outcomes. This subchapter aims to delve into the influence of political parties on electoral outcomes, focusing on the interplay between controversial ideologies and democratic processes. By examining case studies such as the elections of Hamas in Palestine, Ortega in Nicaragua, Allende in Chile, and Carter and Biden in the United States, this chapter seeks to provide scholars with a comprehensive understanding of the dynamics at play.

The Role of Political Parties in the Democratic Process:

Political parties are vital actors in democratic systems, serving as intermediaries between citizens and government. They shape public opinion, mobilize voters, and articulate policy platforms that appeal to specific constituencies. The choices made by political parties can sway electoral outcomes, as seen in the election of leaders with controversial ideologies. Understanding the role of political parties is crucial for comprehending the complexities of democratic processes.

The Impact of Socioeconomic Factors on Electoral Outcomes:

Socioeconomic factors, such as income inequality, poverty rates, and unemployment, often influence electoral outcomes. Political parties that effectively address these concerns and propose viable solutions tend to gain support from the electorate. This subchapter explores the connection between socioeconomic factors and the rise of populist leaders in democratic societies, offering insights into how these factors shape electoral choices.

Assessing the Consequences of Electing Leaders with Controversial Ideologies:

Elections that result in the victory of leaders with controversial ideologies raise important questions about the consequences for democracy. By analyzing case studies, this subchapter will evaluate the short-term and long-term effects of electing leaders with socialist or leftist agendas, shedding light on the challenges and opportunities presented by these electoral outcomes.

Analyzing the Relationship between Democracy and Radical Political Movements:

Democracy faces the challenge of striking a balance between inclusivity and the rise of radical political movements. This subchapter explores the relationship between democracy and radical ideologies, investigating how the democratic process can be influenced by extreme political movements. Understanding this dynamic is crucial for scholars seeking to assess the compatibility of controversial ideologies with democratic systems.

Conclusion:

This subchapter has provided an in-depth analysis of the influence of political parties on electoral outcomes. By examining case studies, exploring socioeconomic factors, and assessing the consequences of electing leaders with controversial ideologies, scholars gain valuable insights into the complexities of democratic processes. Furthermore, this subchapter addresses the challenges faced by democracies in managing political transitions and maintaining stability during times of political polarization. By understanding the interplay between political parties and electoral outcomes, scholars can contribute to the ongoing discourse on controversial ideologies in power and their impact on democracy.

Chapter 3: The Impact of Socioeconomic Factors on Electoral Outcomes

Income Inequality and Voting Patterns

Income inequality is a pressing issue that has significant implications for democratic societies. This subchapter delves into the relationship between income inequality and voting patterns, shedding light on how socioeconomic factors shape electoral outcomes. Scholars and individuals interested in the impact of income inequality on democracy will find this analysis particularly insightful.

One of the key findings in this subchapter is the close link between income inequality and the rise of populist leaders in democratic societies. As income inequality increases, disenfranchised citizens often turn to charismatic leaders who promise to address their grievances and bridge the wealth gap. The electoral outcomes of several countries, such as the election of Hamas in Palestine, Ortega in Nicaragua, Allende in Chile, and Carter and Biden in the United States, serve as case studies to explore this phenomenon.

Moreover, the subchapter examines the consequences of electing leaders with controversial ideologies, particularly those with socialist or leftist agendas. It assesses the long-term effects of such leaders on democratic systems, considering both the positive and negative ramifications. By analyzing historical examples and conducting comparative studies, scholars can gain a comprehensive understanding of the challenges and opportunities presented by leaders with controversial ideologies.

The impact of income inequality on voter behavior is another significant aspect explored in this subchapter. Socioeconomic factors, such as wealth disparities, educational attainment, and social mobility, play a crucial role in shaping voting patterns. By studying these factors, scholars can assess the efficacy of democratic systems in managing political transitions and maintaining stability during times of polarization.

Foreign interference in democratic elections is also investigated, as it has become an increasingly prevalent concern. Understanding the role of external actors in shaping electoral outcomes is crucial for scholars studying the integrity and resilience of democratic processes.

Overall, this subchapter offers a comprehensive analysis of the relationship between income inequality and voting patterns in democratic societies. By exploring the impact of socioeconomic factors, the rise of populist leaders, the consequences of controversial ideologies, and the challenges faced by democracies, scholars can gain valuable insights into the complex dynamics of democratic systems. This analysis is essential for individuals interested in the functioning and stability of democratic societies and provides a foundation for further research and discussion.

Education and Political Preferences

Education plays a crucial role in shaping individuals' political preferences and ideologies. This subchapter explores the complex relationship between education and political choices, shedding light on how educational attainment influences democratic outcomes and the rise of controversial ideologies. Drawing upon case studies from different countries, this chapter aims to provide scholars with a comprehensive understanding of the impact of education on political preferences.

One of the key observations is the correlation between higher levels of education and more liberal political leanings. Numerous studies have shown that individuals with higher education tend to support progressive policies, embrace diversity, and advocate for social justice. This phenomenon can be attributed to the exposure to diverse perspectives, critical thinking skills, and the development of a broader worldview that education fosters.

However, it is important to note that education's influence on political preferences is not uniform across all societies. The impact of education can vary depending on cultural, socioeconomic, and historical factors. For example, in some societies, education may reinforce conservative values and ideologies due to the influence of traditional norms and religious beliefs.

Furthermore, the quality of education also plays a significant role. Disparities in educational resources and opportunities can lead to unequal political participation and biased preferences. Therefore, addressing educational inequalities is crucial to ensure that citizens have access to unbiased information and critical thinking skills necessary for informed political decision-making.

The subchapter also delves into the role of education in countering radical political movements. Education is a powerful tool in promoting democratic values, fostering tolerance, and challenging extremist ideologies. By equipping individuals with the knowledge and skills to critically analyze political rhetoric and propaganda, education can contribute to the resilience of democratic systems.

However, the chapter also acknowledges the potential challenges and limitations of education in countering controversial ideologies. In some cases, education may inadvertently contribute to the polarization of societies by reinforcing pre-existing biases and prejudices. Therefore, it is essential to adopt inclusive and comprehensive educational approaches that encourage open-mindedness, critical thinking, and respectful dialogue.

Overall, this subchapter highlights the intricate relationship between education and political preferences. It underscores the importance of equitable access to quality education as a means to empower citizens, promote democratic values, and mitigate the risks associated with the rise of controversial ideologies. By understanding the dynamics between education and political choices, scholars can contribute to the development of effective strategies to strengthen democratic systems and ensure their sustainability in an ever-changing world.

Unemployment and Voting Behavior

Introduction:

In the realm of democratic elections, the relationship between unemployment and voting behavior has been a subject of great interest and debate. This subchapter aims to delve into the intricate dynamics that exist between these two factors and shed light on their impact on democracy. By exploring various case studies and analyzing the role of socioeconomic factors, this chapter seeks to offer a comprehensive understanding of how unemployment shapes voter behavior and influences electoral outcomes.

Unemployment as a Political Catalyst:

Unemployment is a potent force that has the potential to sway voter sentiments and electoral outcomes. When democracies grapple with high unemployment rates, citizens often become disillusioned with the incumbent government's ability to address their economic concerns. This discontent can lead to a surge in support for alternative political parties or candidates who promise tangible solutions to unemployment and economic woes.

Case Studies:

Examining historical cases, such as the election of Hamas in Palestine, Ortega in Nicaragua, Allende in Chile, and the election of Carter and Biden in the United States, we can identify patterns in voter behavior during times of economic hardship. These instances provide valuable insights into the complex relationship between unemployment and voting behavior.

The Impact of Socioeconomic Factors:

While unemployment undoubtedly influences voting behavior, it is crucial to recognize that socioeconomic factors play a significant role as well. Income inequality, access to education, and social mobility all contribute to shaping voter preferences. By studying these factors, scholars can gain a deeper understanding of why certain segments of society are more inclined to support radical or populist leaders during times of economic uncertainty.

Long-Term Effects and Consequences:

The consequences of electing leaders with controversial ideologies, particularly those with socialist or leftist agendas, can have lasting effects on the political and economic landscape of a country. This subchapter will explore the long-term effects of such electoral choices, including the challenges faced by democracies in maintaining stability during times of political polarization.

Conclusion:

Unemployment and its impact on voting behavior are crucial aspects to consider when assessing the health and functioning of a democratic system. By analyzing case studies, socioeconomic factors, and the long-term consequences of electing leaders with controversial ideologies, scholars can gain valuable insights into the challenges faced by democracies worldwide. Understanding these dynamics is essential for maintaining stability, promoting social cohesion, and ensuring the effective management of political transitions in democratic societies.

Chapter 4: The Rise of Populist Leaders in Democratic Societies

Defining Populism and its Characteristics

Populism has emerged as a significant and controversial political ideology in several democratic societies across the globe. In order to understand its impact on democracy, it is essential to define populism and explore its characteristics. This subchapter aims to provide a comprehensive analysis of populism, its origins, and the key features that define this ideology.

Populism refers to a political approach that claims to represent the interests of ordinary people against a perceived corrupt elite. It is characterized by a charismatic leader who establishes a direct and emotional connection with the masses, often bypassing traditional political parties and institutions. Populists tend to simplify complex issues, offering straightforward solutions to socio-economic problems.

One of the defining characteristics of populism is its focus on the people as a unified and homogeneous entity. Populist leaders often create a dichotomy between the "ordinary people" and the "corrupt elite" or "establishment." They project themselves as the saviors of the people, promising to restore their sovereignty and protect their interests.

Another key aspect of populism is its anti-establishment rhetoric. Populist leaders often criticize and challenge the existing political order, claiming that it has failed to address the concerns of the people. They capitalize on public frustration and disillusionment with the mainstream political parties, portraying themselves as the voice of the forgotten and marginalized.

Populist movements also tend to exhibit a strong nationalist or nativist sentiment. They emphasize the protection of national identity, culture, and values, often at the expense of minority groups or immigrants. This emphasis on national sovereignty and protectionism resonates with segments of the population who feel threatened by globalization and international integration.

Furthermore, populism thrives on polarization and divisiveness. Populist leaders often exploit societal divisions, fueling a sense of "us versus them." They create an adversarial dynamic between the people and the so-called enemies of the nation, fostering a climate of hostility and intolerance.

Understanding these characteristics of populism is crucial in assessing its impact on democracy. Populist leaders can stir up strong emotions and mobilize a significant portion of the population, but their simplistic solutions and divisive rhetoric can also undermine democratic institutions and processes. This subchapter aims to delve into the complexities of populism and shed light on its consequences for democratic societies. By examining case studies and drawing on scholarly research, we can gain insights into the challenges posed by populist ideologies and explore potential strategies to safeguard democracy in the face of populist movements.

Populist Movements and Electoral Success

In recent years, the rise of populist movements and their electoral success has become a topic of great interest and concern among scholars and experts in democracy. This subchapter aims to delve into the complex relationship between populist leaders and democratic systems, exploring the factors that contribute to their rise and the consequences of electing leaders with controversial ideologies.

When examining the electoral success of populist movements, it is essential to consider the role of political parties in the democratic process. These parties act as vehicles for presenting and promoting ideologies to the electorate. By understanding how parties mobilize and communicate their messages, we can better comprehend the appeal of populism to voters in different societies.

Socioeconomic factors also play a critical role in shaping electoral outcomes. Issues such as income inequality, unemployment, and social mobility can create fertile ground for populist rhetoric. By analyzing the impact of these factors, we can gain insights into why certain populations gravitate towards populist leaders and ideologies.

The rise of populist leaders in democratic societies raises questions about the efficacy of democratic systems in managing political transitions. While democracy is often seen as a stabilizing force, the election of leaders with controversial agendas can challenge its core principles. This subchapter will evaluate the consequences of electing such leaders, examining the potential tensions between populism and democratic governance.

Moreover, it is crucial to study the factors influencing voter behavior in democratic elections. Understanding the motivations behind voter choices can shed light on the appeal of populist movements and their success. Factors such as identity politics, economic anxieties, and the role of media and social networks will be analyzed to gain a comprehensive understanding of voter behavior.

In the context of democratic elections, foreign interference has emerged as a significant concern. This subchapter will explore the role of external actors in influencing electoral outcomes, addressing the challenges faced by democracies in safeguarding the integrity of their electoral processes.

Finally, this subchapter will investigate the long-term effects of electing leaders with socialist or leftist agendas. By assessing the economic, social, and political consequences of such leadership, we can better understand the impact on democratic systems and the societies they govern.

In conclusion, the rise of populist movements and their electoral success poses both challenges and opportunities for democratic governance. By examining the factors behind their rise, the consequences of electing leaders with controversial ideologies, and the challenges faced by democracies, scholars can gain valuable insights into the impact of populism on democracy. This subchapter aims to contribute to the ongoing discourse on controversial ideologies in power and their implications for democratic societies.

Populist Leaders and their Impact on Democracy

In recent years, the rise of populist leaders in democratic societies has sparked intense debates and raised concerns among scholars and political commentators. This subchapter delves into the impact of these leaders on democracy, exploring their controversial ideologies and assessing the consequences of electing them into power.

Populist leaders often emerge during times of political polarization, economic uncertainty, and social unrest. They capitalize on the dissatisfaction of the masses, presenting themselves as the voice of the people against an elite establishment. While their rhetoric may resonate with certain segments of the population, their ideologies often challenge the principles and norms that underpin democratic systems.

When examining the impact of populist leaders on democracy, it is essential to consider specific case studies where democratic processes have resulted in the election of leaders with controversial ideologies. For instance, Palestinians elected Hamas, Nicaraguans elected Ortega, Chileans elected Allende, and Americans elected Carter and Biden. These examples highlight the complexities and challenges associated with democratic elections, where the will of the people may not always align with the expectations of scholars and observers.

One key aspect to consider is the role of political parties in the democratic process. Political parties play a crucial role in shaping the electoral landscape and influencing voter behavior. They can either be a vehicle for democratic governance or a conduit for populist movements. Understanding the dynamics between political parties and populist leaders is essential in comprehending the impact on democracy.

Furthermore, the impact of socioeconomic factors on electoral outcomes cannot be underestimated. Economic inequality, social divisions, and the erosion of trust in institutions can create fertile ground for the rise of populist leaders. Exploring these factors and their relationship with democracy is essential for understanding the context in which these leaders emerge.

Assessing the consequences of electing leaders with controversial ideologies is another crucial aspect of understanding the impact on democracy. Such leaders may implement policies that challenge democratic norms, concentrate power, undermine checks and balances, and limit freedom of speech and press. Scholars must critically analyze the long-term effects of these leaders and their ability to maintain stability during times of political polarization.

In conclusion, the rise of populist leaders in democratic societies poses significant challenges to the functioning of democracy. Understanding their impact requires a multidimensional analysis that considers the role of political parties, socioeconomic factors, and the consequences of electing leaders with controversial ideologies. By critically examining these issues, scholars can contribute to a deeper understanding of the complex relationship between populism and democracy, enabling societies to navigate the challenges that lie ahead.

Chapter 5: Assessing the Consequences of Electing Leaders with Controversial Ideologies

Ideological Shifts and Policy Changes

In the realm of politics, ideological shifts and policy changes hold significant implications for the functioning of democratic systems. This subchapter delves into the intricate dynamics of such shifts and changes, exploring their impact on democracy and the broader society. By examining various case studies and analyzing the underlying factors, this chapter aims to provide scholars with a comprehensive understanding of the consequences that arise when controversial ideologies come to power.

When democracy does not work, as exemplified by the elections of Hamas in Palestine, Ortega in Nicaragua, Allende in Chile, Carter and Biden in the United States, it becomes imperative to assess the role of political parties in the democratic process. These case studies shed light on the complexities of democratic elections and highlight the need to scrutinize the influence and actions of political parties in shaping both policy and ideology.

Furthermore, the impact of socioeconomic factors on electoral outcomes cannot be ignored. This subchapter explores how economic disparities, social inequality, and other socioeconomic factors can sway voter behavior, leading to unexpected electoral results. By studying these factors, scholars can better understand the intricate relationship between socioeconomic context and political outcomes.

One notable trend in recent years has been the rise of populist leaders in democratic societies. This phenomenon has significant implications for democracy, as it challenges established norms and institutions. The subchapter evaluates the rise of populism, its impact on democratic processes, and the consequences of electing leaders with controversial ideologies.

Additionally, it delves into the consequences of electing leaders with socialist or leftist agendas, analyzing the long-term effects on society and the economy. By examining cases such as those of Allende in Chile, this subchapter provides a nuanced assessment of the challenges and outcomes associated with electing leaders who champion radical ideologies.

Examining the relationship between democracy and radical political movements is another crucial aspect of this subchapter. By analyzing historical examples, scholars can gain insights into the complexities of managing political transitions and the efficacy of democratic systems in such contexts.

Voter behavior in democratic elections is influenced by a myriad of factors, including media, propaganda, and foreign interference. This subchapter investigates the role of these factors and their impact on electoral outcomes, shedding light on the challenges faced by democracies in maintaining stability during times of political polarization.

In conclusion, "Ideological Shifts and Policy Changes" provides a comprehensive analysis of the impact of controversial ideologies on democracy. By examining various case studies and exploring the multifaceted factors influencing electoral outcomes, this subchapter equips scholars with a deeper understanding of the challenges and consequences associated with electing leaders with controversial agendas.

Social Polarization and Divisions

In the realm of democratic governance, social polarization and divisions have emerged as pressing challenges that demand our attention. This subchapter aims to delve into the complexities of this issue, exploring its causes, consequences, and potential solutions. Addressed primarily to scholars, this content seeks to provide a comprehensive understanding of social polarization and divisions in democratic societies.

At its core, social polarization refers to the deepening divides within a society, often along political, ethnic, religious, or socioeconomic lines. These divisions can be fueled by various factors, such as economic inequality, cultural differences, and political grievances. Understanding the root causes of social polarization is crucial to comprehending its impact on democracy.

This subchapter will shed light on the consequences of social polarization and divisions in the context of democratic processes. It will examine how these divisions can fragment societies, erode trust in democratic institutions, and hinder effective governance. Additionally, it will explore the rise of populist leaders in democratic societies and their relationship with social polarization, emphasizing the potential threats they pose to democratic norms and values.

An analysis of the relationship between democracy and radical political movements will further elucidate the challenges faced by democracies in managing political transitions. By examining case studies such as the rise of Hamas in Palestine, Ortega in Nicaragua, Allende in Chile, and Carter and Biden in the United States, this subchapter aims to assess the consequences of electing leaders with controversial ideologies. It will delve into the long-term effects of electing leaders with socialist or leftist agendas, evaluating their impact on political stability, economic development, and individual freedoms.

Moreover, this content will explore the factors influencing voter behavior in democratic elections, including the role of political parties and the impact of socioeconomic factors on electoral outcomes. It will also delve into the challenges faced by democracies in maintaining stability during times of political polarization, considering the role of foreign interference and analyzing strategies to mitigate its effects.

In conclusion, this subchapter offers an in-depth examination of social polarization and divisions in democratic societies. By addressing the complexities and consequences of this issue, it aims to contribute to the scholarly discourse surrounding the challenges faced by democracies worldwide. By engaging with these topics, scholars can gain valuable insights into the factors that shape electoral outcomes, the rise of populist leaders, and the challenges that democracies encounter in maintaining stability during times of political polarization.

International Relations and Diplomatic Challenges

In today's globalized world, international relations and diplomatic challenges play a crucial role in shaping the course of democracies across the globe. The interactions between nation-states and the diplomatic efforts undertaken by governments have a significant impact on the functioning and stability of democratic systems. This subchapter delves into the complex dynamics of international relations and the diplomatic challenges faced by democracies, with a focus on controversial ideologies in power.

When democracy does not work, the consequences can be far-reaching. We have witnessed instances where democratically elected leaders with controversial ideologies have come to power. Palestinians elected Hamas, Nicaraguans elected Ortega, Chileans elected Allende, Americans elected Carter and Biden. These examples raise important questions about the role of political parties in the democratic process and the impact of socioeconomic factors on electoral outcomes. Understanding these factors is crucial for assessing the consequences of electing leaders with controversial ideologies and analyzing the relationship between democracy and radical political movements.

Furthermore, this subchapter explores the efficacy of democratic systems in managing political transitions. Democracies often face challenges in maintaining stability during times of political polarization. The rise of populist leaders in democratic societies has added another layer of complexity to this issue. By studying the factors influencing voter behavior in democratic elections and evaluating the role of foreign interference, scholars can gain insights into the challenges faced by democracies in maintaining stability.

One particular aspect of electing leaders with socialist or leftist agendas has been a subject of debate. Assessing the long-term effects of such elections is essential for understanding the impact on democracy and the broader socio-political landscape. This subchapter investigates the challenges faced by democracies in maintaining stability and addressing the needs of their citizens when leaders with controversial ideologies are in power.

In conclusion, international relations and diplomatic challenges have a profound impact on the functioning and stability of democracies. This subchapter provides scholars with a comprehensive exploration of various aspects related to controversial ideologies in power. By analyzing the relationship between democracy and radical political movements, assessing the consequences of electing leaders with controversial ideologies, and evaluating the efficacy of democratic systems in managing political transitions, scholars can gain a deeper understanding of the challenges faced by democracies in maintaining stability during times of political polarization.

Chapter 6: Analyzing the Relationship between Democracy and Radical Political Movements

Radicalism as a Threat to Democracy

Introduction:

In recent times, the rise of radical political movements has posed a significant threat to democratic systems around the world. This subchapter aims to explore the relationship between democracy and radicalism and assess the impact of such ideologies on the democratic process. By analyzing case studies and examining historical events, this chapter aims to shed light on the consequences of electing leaders with controversial ideologies and the challenges faced by democracies in managing political transitions.

Understanding Radicalism:

Radicalism, in the context of this chapter, refers to extreme political ideologies that challenge the fundamental principles of democracy. These ideologies often advocate for revolutionary change, reject the existing political order, and seek to implement their own controversial agendas. Examples of such movements can be found in various countries, including Hamas in Palestine, Ortega in Nicaragua, Allende in Chile, and even leaders like Carter and Biden in the United States.

Impact on Democracy:

When radical leaders are elected into power, the consequences for democracy can be far-reaching. Their controversial agendas often undermine the rule of law, suppress dissent, and curtail individual freedoms. Moreover, radical movements tend to polarize societies, leading to increased tensions and divisions among citizens. This polarization poses a significant challenge to the stability of democratic systems and can hinder effective governance.

Challenges Faced by Democracies:

One of the key challenges faced by democracies is maintaining stability during times of political polarization. Radical movements often exploit such divisions, exacerbating social unrest and undermining democratic institutions. Additionally, the efficacy of democratic systems in managing political transitions is tested when leaders with controversial ideologies come to power. The transition from radicalism to a more moderate political landscape can be turbulent, potentially leading to further social and political instability.

Conclusion:

As this subchapter demonstrates, radicalism poses a considerable threat to democracy. The election of leaders with controversial ideologies can have profound and lasting consequences for the democratic process, as seen in the case studies of Palestine, Nicaragua, Chile, and the United States. It is crucial for scholars and policymakers to critically analyze the factors influencing voter behavior, the impact of socioeconomic factors, and the role of foreign interference in democratic elections. By understanding the relationship between democracy and radical political movements, it becomes possible to assess the efficacy of democratic systems in managing political transitions and maintaining stability during times of polarization. Only through such analysis can we effectively address the challenges faced by democracies and safeguard the principles of democracy in the face of radicalism.

Radical Movements and their Strategies

In the complex landscape of democratic societies, radical movements have emerged as influential players, challenging the traditional political order and, in some cases, even ascending to power. Understanding their strategies and analyzing the consequences of their electoral victories is crucial for scholars and those interested in the functioning of democracy. This subchapter explores the dynamics of radical movements and their impact on democratic systems.

Radical movements, by their nature, advocate for substantial and often drastic changes to the existing social and political structures. They operate on the fringes of mainstream politics, aiming to disrupt the status quo and address perceived injustices. However, their strategies vary, and this chapter delves into the different approaches employed by these movements.

One strategy adopted by radical movements is populism, which capitalizes on the discontentment of marginalized groups. Populist leaders, through charismatic rhetoric and promises of change, appeal to the frustrations of the electorate. This section examines the rise of populist leaders within democratic societies and the implications of their electoral success.

Furthermore, the chapter explores the consequences of electing leaders with controversial ideologies. It delves into case studies such as the election of Hamas in Palestine, Ortega in Nicaragua, Allende in Chile, Carter and Biden in the United States, and evaluates the long-term effects of leaders with socialist or leftist agendas. By analyzing the policies and governance of these leaders, scholars can assess the impact on democratic systems and the broader society.

The relationship between democracy and radical political movements is another focal point. This section investigates the challenges faced by democracies in managing political transitions when radical movements come to power. It also examines the role of political parties in the democratic process, exploring how they can both facilitate and hinder the rise of radical movements.

Moreover, this subchapter delves into the factors influencing voter behavior in democratic elections. It emphasizes the impact of socioeconomic factors on electoral outcomes, as well as the role of foreign interference. By studying these factors, scholars can gain insights into the dynamics of democratic elections and their vulnerability to external influences.

Lastly, the chapter addresses the challenges faced by democracies in maintaining stability during times of political polarization. It investigates the role of radical movements in exacerbating polarization and explores potential strategies for mitigating its effects.

Overall, this subchapter provides a comprehensive analysis of radical movements and their strategies within democratic societies. By examining case studies, evaluating the consequences of electing leaders with controversial ideologies, and exploring the relationship between democracy and radical political movements, scholars can gain a deeper understanding of the impact of these movements on democratic systems and the challenges they pose to stability and governance.

Combating Radicalism while Preserving Democratic Principles

Title: Combating Radicalism while Preserving Democratic Principles

Introduction:

The rise of radical political movements poses a significant challenge to democratic societies around the world. In this subchapter, we will delve into the complex task of combating radicalism while preserving democratic principles. We will explore the critical role that democratic systems play in managing political transitions and discuss the factors influencing voter behavior in democratic elections. Furthermore, we will analyze the relationship between democracy and radical political movements, assessing the consequences of electing leaders with controversial ideologies.

Preserving Democratic Values:

Democracy is built on the principles of pluralism, freedom of speech, and respect for human rights. To combat radicalism effectively, it is essential to uphold these values. However, striking a balance between preserving democratic principles and countering radical ideologies can be challenging. It requires a multi-faceted approach that includes education, dialogue, and fostering inclusive political environments.

The Role of Political Parties:

Political parties play a crucial role in shaping the democratic process. They act as mediators between citizens and the government, articulating various interests and providing platforms for political debate. Understanding the impact of political parties on electoral outcomes is vital in combating radicalism. By promoting transparency, accountability, and inclusivity within parties, democratic systems can better resist the influence of radical ideologies.

The Threat of Socioeconomic Factors:

Socioeconomic factors can significantly influence electoral outcomes and contribute to the rise of radical movements. Economic inequality, unemployment, and social exclusion can create fertile ground for radicalization. Addressing these socio-economic challenges through targeted policies and inclusive economic development becomes crucial to combat radicalism effectively.

Managing Political Transitions:

The efficacy of democratic systems in managing political transitions plays a pivotal role in preventing radical ideologies from gaining traction. By ensuring a smooth and inclusive transition of power, democratic societies can minimize the chances of radical movements exploiting political vacuums or disenfranchised populations.

Foreign Interference and Radicalism:

Foreign interference in democratic elections can pose a severe threat to democratic principles. Investigating the role of foreign interference in influencing voter behavior and supporting radical movements becomes essential to safeguard democracy. Strengthening cybersecurity measures, promoting media literacy, and enhancing international cooperation are key strategies to counter external interference.

Conclusion:

Combating radicalism while preserving democratic principles is an intricate and urgent task. Democratic societies must address socioeconomic factors, strengthen political parties, and manage political transitions effectively. By analyzing the consequences of electing leaders with controversial ideologies and understanding the relationship between democracy and radical political movements, scholars can contribute to formulating effective strategies to maintain stability during times of political polarization. Upholding democratic values, fostering inclusive political environments, and engaging in international cooperation are vital to ensuring the long-term success of democratic systems in countering the threats posed by radical ideologies.

Chapter 7: Evaluating the Efficacy of Democratic Systems in Managing Political Transitions

Democratic Transitions and Challenges

Introduction

The process of democratic transition is a complex and challenging endeavor that many nations have embarked upon throughout history. This subchapter aims to delve into the various factors and challenges associated with democratic transitions. By examining specific case studies and analyzing the impact of controversial ideologies on democratic systems, this chapter aims to provide scholars with a comprehensive understanding of the intricacies involved in navigating these transitions.

Understanding the Role of Political Parties

One of the crucial aspects of democracy lies in the role of political parties. This section explores how political parties influence and shape the democratic process. By examining the case studies of Palestine, Nicaragua, Chile, the United States, and the challenges faced by each nation in electing leaders such as Hamas, Ortega, Allende, Carter, and Biden, scholars can gain valuable insights into the complexities of democratic transitions.

The Impact of Socioeconomic Factors on Electoral Outcomes

Socioeconomic factors play a significant role in shaping electoral outcomes. This subchapter dives into the relationship between socioeconomic factors and democratic elections. By analyzing how these factors influence voter behavior and electoral outcomes, scholars can gain a deeper understanding of the challenges faced by democracies in managing political transitions.

The Rise of Populist Leaders in Democracies

Populist leaders have emerged as influential figures in democratic societies. This section examines the rise of populist leaders and their impact on democratic systems. By analyzing case studies and assessing the consequences of electing leaders with controversial ideologies, scholars can evaluate the efficacy of democratic systems in managing political transitions.

The Relationship between Democracy and Radical Political Movements

Democratic systems often grapple with the presence of radical political movements. This subchapter explores the relationship between democracy and these movements. By examining case studies and evaluating the challenges faced by democracies in maintaining stability during times of political polarization, scholars can gain insights into the factors influencing voter behavior and the long-term effects of electing leaders with socialist or leftist agendas.

Foreign Interference in Democratic Elections

Foreign interference has become a concerning issue in democratic elections. This section studies the role of foreign interference and its impact on democratic processes. By investigating the challenges faced by democracies and exploring the factors influencing voter behavior, scholars can gain a deeper understanding of the complexities involved in maintaining stable democratic systems.

Conclusion

Democratic transitions are not straightforward processes and are often influenced by various factors, including political parties, socioeconomic conditions, radical political movements, and foreign interference. By analyzing case studies and evaluating the challenges faced by democracies, scholars can gain valuable insights into the intricacies of managing political transitions and maintaining stable democratic systems.

Lessons from Successful Democratic Transitions

Introduction:

In the realm of democratic politics, successful transitions are often regarded as the cornerstone of a stable and prosperous society. While the history of democratic transitions is filled with both triumphs and failures, it is crucial for scholars to learn from the former to understand the dynamics that contribute to successful democratic transitions. This subchapter titled "Lessons from Successful Democratic Transitions" aims to provide valuable insights into this subject matter, drawing from various case studies and scholarly research.

Lessons Learned:

1. The Role of Political Parties: A key lesson from successful democratic transitions is the pivotal role played by political parties. Strong, accountable, and inclusive political parties act as the bedrock of a thriving democracy. They facilitate the formation of stable governments and ensure the representation of diverse interests, thereby contributing to the long-term success of democratic transitions.

2. Impact of Socioeconomic Factors: Socioeconomic factors significantly influence electoral outcomes in democratic transitions. Successful transitions often occur in societies where economic development and social welfare are given priority. Addressing income inequality, improving access to education and healthcare, and providing economic opportunities help build a strong foundation for successful democratic transitions.

3. Managing Political Polarization: Democracies face challenges in maintaining stability during times of political polarization. Successful transitions demonstrate the importance of fostering dialogue, negotiation, and compromise among political actors. Encouraging inclusivity and promoting a sense of national unity can mitigate the

adverse effects of polarization and contribute to the long-term stability of democratic systems.

4. Evaluating Leaders with Controversial Ideologies: Assessing the consequences of electing leaders with controversial ideologies is crucial. Successful democratic transitions highlight the significance of leaders who prioritize democratic values, respect human rights, and uphold the rule of law. A thorough evaluation of leaders' track records and ideologies is necessary to ensure the preservation of democratic principles.

Conclusion:

Lessons from successful democratic transitions provide valuable insights for scholars studying controversial ideologies in power. Understanding the role of political parties, the impact of socioeconomic factors, and the challenges faced during times of political polarization can foster a deeper comprehension of the complexities involved in democratic transitions. By analyzing these lessons, scholars can contribute to the development of strategies and policies that promote the growth and sustainability of democratic systems worldwide.

Pitfalls and Obstacles in Political Transitions

Introduction:

Political transitions are complex processes that involve significant challenges and obstacles. This subchapter aims to critically examine the pitfalls encountered during political transitions and identify the obstacles that hinder the smooth establishment and consolidation of democracy. The analysis focuses on various case studies, such as the election of Hamas in Palestine, Ortega in Nicaragua, Allende in Chile, Carter and Biden in the United States, to shed light on the consequences of electing leaders with controversial ideologies. Moreover, it explores the impact of socioeconomic factors, the rise of populist leaders, and the role of political parties in influencing democratic processes.

Challenges in Political Transitions:

1. Controversial Ideologies: The election of leaders with controversial ideologies can lead to a clash of values and create divisions within society. This can undermine democratic principles and hinder the consolidation of democracy.

2. Socioeconomic Factors: The impact of socioeconomic factors on electoral outcomes cannot be ignored. Economic inequality, poverty, and unemployment can significantly influence voter behavior, leading to the election of leaders with radical agendas.

3. Rise of Populist Leaders: Populist leaders often exploit societal grievances and use divisive rhetoric to gain power. Their rise poses a threat to democratic institutions and can lead to the erosion of democratic norms and values.

4. Role of Political Parties: Political parties play a crucial role in the democratic process. However, when parties prioritize their own interests over the welfare of the nation, it can lead to political polarization and hinder effective political transitions.

5. Foreign Interference: The role of foreign interference in democratic elections has gained attention in recent years. Foreign actors can manipulate the electoral process, undermining the legitimacy of democratic outcomes and destabilizing political transitions.

Conclusion:

Political transitions are intricate processes that require careful navigation to ensure the successful establishment and consolidation of democracy. This subchapter has highlighted the pitfalls and obstacles encountered during political transitions, including the consequences of electing leaders with controversial ideologies, the impact of socioeconomic factors, and the rise of populist leaders. It has also shed light on the role of political parties, foreign interference, and challenges faced by democracies during times of political polarization. By understanding these factors, scholars can gain insights into the complexities of political transitions and contribute to the development of effective strategies for the consolidation of democracy.

Chapter 8: Exploring the Factors Influencing Voter Behavior in Democratic Elections

Political Ideology and Party Affiliation

In the realm of political science, the study of political ideology and party affiliation is crucial for understanding the dynamics of democratic systems. This subchapter delves into the intricate relationship between political ideologies, party affiliations, and their impact on democracy, assessing their consequences and exploring the challenges faced by democracies during times of political polarization.

One key aspect to consider is the role of political parties in the democratic process. Political parties serve as the primary vehicles for organizing and mobilizing citizens, shaping political discourse, and ultimately, competing for power within a democratic system. Understanding how parties align themselves ideologically and how voters affiliate themselves with these parties is essential for comprehending electoral outcomes.

The impact of socioeconomic factors on electoral outcomes cannot be underestimated. Income inequality, unemployment rates, and access to education are just a few examples of socioeconomic factors that can influence voter behavior. By examining these factors, scholars can gain insights into why certain political ideologies or parties resonate more strongly with specific segments of the population.

In recent years, the rise of populist leaders in democratic societies has garnered significant attention. This phenomenon raises questions about the compatibility of populism with democratic principles. Scholars must analyze the origins and consequences of these populist movements, as well as their potential to reshape democratic systems.

Furthermore, assessing the consequences of electing leaders with controversial ideologies is of utmost importance. Case studies such as the election of Hamas in Palestine, Ortega in Nicaragua, Allende in Chile, Carter and Biden in the United States provide valuable insights into the long-term effects of electing leaders with socialist or leftist agendas. By examining these cases, scholars can evaluate the impact of these ideologies on governance, socioeconomic policies, and the overall health of democratic institutions.

Foreign interference in democratic elections has become a growing concern in recent years. Studying the role of foreign actors in influencing electoral outcomes is crucial for safeguarding the integrity of democratic processes. Scholars must explore the methods employed by foreign entities and assess the effectiveness of countermeasures to mitigate their interference.

Lastly, this subchapter investigates the challenges faced by democracies in maintaining stability during times of political polarization. As societies become increasingly divided along ideological lines, the ability of democratic systems to navigate these divisions and preserve stability is put to the test. Analyzing the factors contributing to polarization and evaluating strategies for managing it are essential for the continued success of democratic governance.

In conclusion, this subchapter explores the multifaceted relationship between political ideology, party affiliation, and democracy. By examining the impact of socioeconomic factors, the rise of populist leaders, and the consequences of electing leaders with controversial ideologies, scholars can gain a deeper understanding of the challenges and opportunities that democracy presents. Moreover, studying voter behavior, foreign interference, and the challenges of political polarization provides valuable insights into the efficacy of democratic systems in managing political transitions and maintaining stability.

Media Influence on Voter Choices

Introduction:

In today's digital age, media plays a significant role in shaping public opinion and influencing voter choices. This subchapter aims to explore the impact of media on democratic elections, particularly focusing on the relationship between media and voter behavior. By analyzing the various ways in which media influences voter choices, we can gain a deeper understanding of the challenges faced by democracies in maintaining stability during times of political polarization.

Media as an Agenda Setter:

The media serves as a powerful agenda setter, capable of shaping public discourse and influencing voter perceptions. Through selective coverage, framing, and sensationalism, media outlets can shape the narrative surrounding political candidates and issues. By emphasizing certain aspects and downplaying others, media can sway voter opinion and potentially alter electoral outcomes.

Media Bias and Partisanship:

Media bias and partisanship have become pervasive in democratic societies. Scholars have long debated the extent to which media outlets align with specific political ideologies, leading to divided audiences consuming news from sources that reinforce their pre-existing beliefs. This echo chamber effect can contribute to political polarization and further entrench partisan divisions.

Dissemination of Misinformation:

The rise of social media platforms has amplified the spread of misinformation, posing a significant threat to the integrity of democratic elections. False or misleading information can easily go viral, influencing voter choices and distorting public discourse. Scholars must investigate the role of media in disseminating misinformation and its impact on voter behavior.

Foreign Interference:

The role of foreign interference in democratic elections has gained attention in recent years. Media platforms can be used as tools for spreading propaganda and disinformation campaigns, aiming to influence voter choices and undermine democratic processes. Scholars must assess the extent to which foreign interference through media manipulation impacts electoral outcomes.

Media Literacy and Voter Education:

To counter the potentially negative influence of media on voter choices, promoting media literacy and voter education is crucial. Scholarly research should focus on developing strategies to enhance critical thinking skills among voters, enabling them to discern credible sources and evaluate information objectively.

Conclusion:

Understanding the influence of media on voter choices is essential in assessing the impact of media on democratic processes. By examining media bias, the dissemination of misinformation, foreign interference, and the role of media literacy, scholars can contribute to the development of effective strategies to enhance democratic stability and promote informed voter choices. It is imperative to address these challenges to ensure the integrity and vitality of democratic elections in the face of growing polarization and evolving media landscapes.

Demographic Factors and Voting Patterns

Democracy is a complex and multifaceted system, and understanding the factors that influence voting patterns is crucial to comprehend its functioning. One significant aspect that shapes electoral outcomes is demographic factors. These factors, such as age, gender, ethnicity, and social class, play a pivotal role in determining how individuals vote and which ideologies they align themselves with. In this subchapter, we will delve into the intricate relationship between demographic factors and voting patterns, shedding light on the impact they have on the democratic process.

When examining the impact of demographic factors on electoral outcomes, it becomes evident that different groups within society often exhibit distinct voting patterns. Scholars have extensively studied these patterns to gain insights into the dynamics of democracy. For example, research has shown that older voters tend to lean towards conservative ideologies, while younger voters are more likely to support progressive or liberal candidates. Similarly, gender can influence voting choices, with women historically favoring candidates and policies that prioritize social welfare and equality.

Furthermore, socioeconomic factors also play a crucial role in shaping voting patterns. Income inequality, educational attainment, and employment opportunities can significantly influence how individuals vote. Those facing economic hardships may be more inclined to support candidates who promise economic reforms and social welfare programs. On the other hand, individuals with higher socioeconomic status may favor candidates who focus on fiscal responsibility and market-oriented policies.

Demographic factors also intersect with the rise of populist leaders in democratic societies. Populist movements often target specific segments of the population, appealing to their grievances and fears. By understanding the demographic composition of these movements' support base, scholars can gain valuable insights into the factors that contribute to their success or failure.

Moreover, the consequences of electing leaders with controversial ideologies are also tied to demographic factors. Understanding the demographic makeup of those who support such leaders can help assess the long-term effects of their policies and ideologies on society.

In conclusion, demographic factors are essential in understanding voting patterns and the functioning of democracy. By analyzing the relationship between these factors and electoral outcomes, scholars can gain valuable insights into the challenges faced by democracies, the factors influencing voter behavior, and the impact of electing leaders with controversial ideologies. This subchapter aims to provide a comprehensive examination of the intricate connections between demographic factors and voting patterns, contributing to the broader discourse on the efficacy of democratic systems and the challenges they face in maintaining stability during times of political polarization.

Chapter 9: Studying the Role of Foreign Interference in Democratic Elections

Forms of Foreign Interference

Introduction

Foreign interference in democratic elections is a complex and multifaceted phenomenon that has the potential to disrupt the integrity of democratic systems. This subchapter aims to explore the various forms of foreign interference and their impact on democracy. Understanding these forms is crucial for scholars studying the challenges faced by democracies in maintaining stability during times of political polarization.

1. Cyber Interference

One of the most prevalent forms of foreign interference is cyber interference, which involves the use of digital technologies to manipulate public opinion and influence electoral outcomes. State-sponsored hacking, social media manipulation, and dissemination of false information are some of the tactics employed. Scholars must analyze the role of foreign actors in exploiting digital platforms to influence voter behavior and shape electoral outcomes.

2. Financial Interference

Another form of foreign interference is financial interference, where foreign entities provide financial support to political candidates or parties to influence their policies and actions. This can range from campaign contributions to funding for political advertisements and media campaigns. Scholars must assess the impact of such financial support on the democratic process and the potential for foreign interests to undermine the will of the people.

3. Covert Operations

Foreign interference can also take the form of covert operations, where intelligence agencies or other state actors engage in espionage, sabotage, or manipulation of electoral processes. This includes activities such as hacking into electoral systems, spreading disinformation, and even manipulating voting results. Scholars should delve into the implications of such covert operations for democratic legitimacy and the challenges they pose for maintaining stability.

4. Diplomatic Interference

Diplomatic interference occurs when foreign governments use their diplomatic channels to influence domestic political affairs. This can involve pressuring political leaders, promoting certain ideologies, or even threatening economic sanctions. Scholars must study the impact of such interference on the democratic process and the extent to which it infringes on the sovereignty of nations.

Conclusion

Foreign interference in democratic elections manifests in various forms and poses significant challenges to the democratic process. Scholars must analyze these forms to understand the implications for democracy and the stability of nations. By studying the relationship between foreign interference and democratic systems, scholars can contribute to developing strategies to safeguard the integrity of elections and ensure the continued functioning of democratic societies.

Motivations and Strategies of Foreign Actors

In the realm of democratic politics, the role of foreign actors cannot be underestimated. The motivations and strategies employed by these external forces can have a profound impact on the outcomes of elections and the overall democratic process. Understanding these dynamics is crucial for scholars studying the challenges faced by democracies in maintaining stability during times of political polarization.

Foreign actors often have a vested interest in influencing the outcome of democratic elections. This can be driven by a variety of motivations, including geopolitical considerations, economic interests, or ideological alignments. For example, powerful nations may seek to promote leaders who are more favorable to their own political and economic agendas, thus ensuring their influence over key decision-making processes.

Strategies employed by foreign actors to influence democratic elections can range from overt interference to more subtle forms of influence. Traditional methods such as covert funding of political parties or candidates, spreading disinformation or propaganda, and engaging in cyberattacks to disrupt the electoral process have all been utilized. In recent years, we have also witnessed the use of social media platforms to manipulate public opinion and sway electoral outcomes.

The impact of foreign interference on democratic elections is a subject of great concern. It raises questions about the integrity of the democratic process and the ability of citizens to make informed decisions. It also highlights the vulnerability of democracies to external manipulation and the need for robust safeguards to protect against such interference.

Scholars studying the relationship between democracy and radical political movements must also consider the role of foreign actors. These actors can provide support, both overt and covert, to radical groups that seek to challenge democratic norms and institutions. Understanding the motivations and strategies employed by foreign actors in supporting these movements is crucial for assessing the consequences of electing leaders with controversial ideologies.

In conclusion, the motivations and strategies of foreign actors in democratic politics are multifaceted and complex. Scholars studying the challenges faced by democracies in maintaining stability during times of political polarization must consider the role of external forces. By examining the impact of foreign interference on electoral outcomes and the relationship between democracy and radical political movements, we can gain a better understanding of the efficacy of democratic systems in managing political transitions. Furthermore, exploring the factors influencing voter behavior and assessing the long-term effects of electing leaders with controversial ideologies can contribute to a more comprehensive understanding of the dynamics at play in democratic politics.

Safeguarding Democratic Elections against Foreign Interference

In today's interconnected world, safeguarding democratic elections against foreign interference has become a pressing concern for scholars studying the impact of controversial ideologies on democracy. The rise of globalization and advancements in technology have created new opportunities for foreign actors to influence electoral outcomes, posing a threat to the integrity of democratic processes.

Foreign interference in democratic elections can take various forms, such as cyberattacks, disinformation campaigns, and financial support to political candidates. These interventions aim to manipulate public opinion, undermine trust in democratic institutions, and ultimately sway the outcome of elections. Scholars researching the role of political parties in the democratic process must address this growing challenge to ensure the integrity and fairness of elections.

The impact of socioeconomic factors on electoral outcomes cannot be fully understood without considering the potential influence of foreign interference. It is essential to assess the extent to which external actors exploit existing socioeconomic divisions to further their own agendas and manipulate electoral results.

Furthermore, the rise of populist leaders in democratic societies has created fertile ground for foreign interference. Scholars exploring the consequences of electing leaders with controversial ideologies should analyze the potential role played by external actors in supporting and amplifying these leaders' narratives and policies.

The relationship between democracy and radical political movements is also susceptible to foreign interference. Scholars must delve into the dynamics of how external actors exploit radical movements to destabilize democratic processes, leading to potential erosion of democratic norms and institutions.

Evaluating the efficacy of democratic systems in managing political transitions is incomplete without considering the challenges posed by foreign interference. External actors may seek to exploit vulnerabilities during these delicate periods to influence the direction and outcome of political transitions.

Foreign interference in democratic elections also impacts voter behavior. Scholars studying the factors influencing voter behavior in democratic elections should examine the ways in which external actors shape public opinion through disinformation and propaganda campaigns.

To assess the long-term effects of electing leaders with socialist or leftist agendas, scholars must analyze the potential role of foreign interference in amplifying or distorting the impacts of such policies. Understanding the influence of external actors is crucial to comprehensively evaluating the consequences of controversial ideologies in power.

Lastly, investigating the challenges faced by democracies in maintaining stability during times of political polarization should include an examination of how foreign interference exacerbates divisions and further polarizes societies.

In conclusion, safeguarding democratic elections against foreign interference is an essential concern for scholars studying controversial ideologies in power. By addressing this challenge, scholars can contribute to the development of effective strategies and policies to uphold the integrity of democratic processes and preserve the fundamental principles of democracy.

Chapter 10: Assessing the Long-Term Effects of Electing Leaders with Socialist or Leftist Agendas

Economic Policies and their Impact on Society

In this subchapter, we delve into the intricate relationship between economic policies and their profound impact on society. As scholars exploring the controversial ideologies in power and their effects on democracy, it is essential to understand the role of economic policies in shaping societal dynamics.

When democracy does not work, as evidenced by the election of leaders such as Hamas in Palestine, Ortega in Nicaragua, Allende in Chile, Carter, and Biden in the United States, it becomes imperative to analyze the influence of economic policies on electoral outcomes. Economic factors, such as unemployment rates, income inequality, and access to basic services, play a significant role in shaping voter behavior and determining election results. By studying the impact of socioeconomic factors on electoral outcomes, we can gain valuable insights into the relationship between economic policies and democracy.

One notable phenomenon observed in recent years is the rise of populist leaders in democratic societies. These leaders often employ controversial ideologies and propose economic policies that resonate with the grievances of a significant portion of the population. It is crucial to assess the consequences of electing such leaders, as their policies may have far-reaching implications for democracy and societal stability.

Moreover, this subchapter explores the efficacy of democratic systems in managing political transitions. Political transitions, especially during times of polarization, pose significant challenges to democracies. By evaluating the efficacy of democratic systems in managing these transitions, scholars can gain insights into potential improvements or reforms necessary to maintain stability.

Additionally, this subchapter examines the factors influencing voter behavior in democratic elections. Socioeconomic factors, media influence, political party affiliations, and foreign interference are all aspects that shape voter choices. By studying these factors, we can gain a comprehensive understanding of the complexities surrounding democratic elections.

Furthermore, we investigate the long-term effects of electing leaders with socialist or leftist agendas. By analyzing the socioeconomic outcomes in countries that have elected such leaders, we can assess the benefits and challenges associated with these ideologies.

Lastly, this subchapter explores the challenges faced by democracies in maintaining stability during times of political polarization. Political polarization can often lead to societal divisions, which in turn threaten democracy. Understanding the factors contributing to political polarization and exploring strategies to mitigate its negative consequences is crucial for scholars studying the impact of economic policies on society.

In conclusion, this subchapter delves into the multifaceted relationship between economic policies and their impact on society. By analyzing the influence of economic policies on electoral outcomes, assessing the consequences of controversial ideologies, and exploring the challenges faced by democracies, scholars can gain valuable insights into the complex dynamics of democracy in the face of economic policies.

Redistribution of Wealth and Social Equality

In the quest for a fair and just society, the redistribution of wealth and pursuit of social equality have emerged as prominent topics in contemporary political discourse. This subchapter delves into the complexities and implications of these concepts, as well as their impact on democracy.

The notion of redistribution of wealth revolves around the idea of addressing economic disparities by reallocating resources from the wealthy to the less privileged. Proponents argue that this approach can rectify historical inequalities and promote social cohesion. However, critics caution that excessive redistribution may stifle individual incentives and hinder economic growth.

Social equality, on the other hand, encompasses a broader range of dimensions beyond wealth distribution. It aims to eliminate societal barriers based on factors such as race, gender, and ethnicity, fostering equal opportunities and outcomes for all citizens. Achieving social equality necessitates not only economic reforms but also comprehensive policies addressing education, healthcare, and access to justice.

Within the context of democracy, the question arises: how does the pursuit of redistribution of wealth and social equality impact the functioning of democratic systems? Proponents argue that these measures help mitigate social unrest, enhance social mobility, and strengthen the democratic fabric. They assert that reducing economic disparities and promoting social equality are essential for a thriving democracy with an engaged and empowered citizenry.

However, critics contend that excessive redistribution may undermine individual liberties and property rights, leading to a concentration of power in the hands of the state. They caution that an overreliance on government intervention may impede economic productivity, discourage innovation, and weaken the overall competitiveness of a nation.

In order to assess the impact of redistribution of wealth and social equality on democracy, it is crucial to examine case studies where leaders with controversial ideologies have championed these causes. Analyzing the consequences of electing such leaders, both in the short and long term, can provide valuable insights into the efficacy and sustainability of their policies.

Moreover, this subchapter explores the challenges faced by democracies in maintaining stability during times of political polarization, as debates surrounding redistribution of wealth and social equality often fuel ideological divisions. It also investigates the factors influencing voter behavior in democratic elections, including the role of foreign interference, as well as the efficacy of democratic systems in managing political transitions.

By critically examining the relationship between redistribution of wealth, social equality, and democracy, this subchapter aims to contribute to the scholarly discourse on controversial ideologies in power. It seeks to provide a comprehensive understanding of the implications of these concepts, enabling scholars to assess their impact on democratic systems and the challenges they pose to maintaining stability and inclusivity in society.

Social Programs and their Sustainability

In recent years, the sustainability and effectiveness of social programs have become topics of great importance in democratic societies. Scholars have examined the impact of these programs on democracy, seeking to understand their role in shaping electoral outcomes and the overall stability of a nation. This subchapter delves into the complexities surrounding social programs and their long-term viability, shedding light on the challenges faced by democracies in maintaining stability during times of political polarization.

One of the key aspects to consider is the relationship between social programs and voter behavior. Socioeconomic factors play a significant role in electoral outcomes, as citizens often vote based on their perceived economic interests. Understanding the impact of these factors is crucial in evaluating the efficacy of democratic systems in managing political transitions. This subchapter explores the factors influencing voter behavior in democratic elections, providing insight into the role social programs play in shaping political landscapes.

Additionally, this subchapter examines the consequences of electing leaders with controversial ideologies, particularly those with socialist or leftist agendas. The long-term effects of such leaders on the sustainability of social programs are assessed, taking into account the potential challenges faced by democracies in maintaining stability. By investigating the efficacy of these programs under different political ideologies, scholars can gain a deeper understanding of their impact on democracy.

Foreign interference in democratic elections has become a growing concern in recent years. This subchapter also explores the role of foreign interference in shaping electoral outcomes and its potential impact on the sustainability of social programs. By studying the extent of foreign influence, scholars can better assess the vulnerabilities of democracies and propose strategies to safeguard against such interference.

Ultimately, this subchapter aims to provide scholars with a comprehensive analysis of social programs and their sustainability within the context of democratic societies. By addressing the challenges faced by democracies, the impact of controversial ideologies, and the role of socioeconomic factors, this subchapter offers valuable insights into the complexities of managing social programs in an ever-changing political landscape. Through careful examination and analysis, scholars can contribute to the ongoing discourse on how to effectively maintain stability and promote the sustainability of social programs in democratic societies.

Chapter 11: Investigating the Challenges Faced by Democracies in Maintaining Stability during Times of Political Polarization

Polarization and its Consequences

In the realm of democratic politics, polarization refers to the growing division and ideological distance between different segments of society. It is a phenomenon that has gained significant attention in recent years due to its far-reaching consequences on the functioning and stability of democratic systems. In this subchapter, we will delve into the concept of polarization and explore its multifaceted consequences on both domestic and international politics.

One of the immediate consequences of polarization is the fracturing of societies into opposing ideological camps. This can lead to increased hostility, animosity, and a breakdown of civil discourse. When democracy does not work, and polarization intensifies, we witness instances where controversial leaders with radical ideologies are elected into power. Examples include the election of Hamas in Palestine, Ortega in Nicaragua, Allende in Chile, as well as Carter and Biden in the United States.

Political parties play a pivotal role in the democratic process, and polarization often deepens the divide between them. This subchapter will explore the impact of polarization on political parties and their ability to effectively represent the diverse interests of the electorate.

Moreover, socioeconomic factors have been found to influence electoral outcomes, and this influence is often exacerbated in times of polarization. We will examine how socioeconomic factors interact with polarization to shape electoral choices and outcomes.

The rise of populist leaders, who exploit the divisions within society, is another consequence of polarization. We will analyze this phenomenon in democratic societies and explore the reasons behind the growing appeal of populist rhetoric.

Electing leaders with controversial ideologies can have far-reaching consequences for a democracy. This subchapter will assess the impact of such leaders on democratic institutions, civil liberties, and social cohesion.

Furthermore, we will investigate the intricate relationship between democracy and radical political movements. How do these movements emerge, and what challenges do they pose to democratic systems?

Transition periods in politics are often characterized by heightened polarization. We will evaluate the efficacy of democratic systems in managing political transitions and maintaining stability during times of polarization.

Voter behavior is influenced by a multitude of factors, and polarization has been proven to be one of them. We will study the factors that influence voter behavior and how polarization shapes electoral outcomes.

Additionally, foreign interference in democratic elections has become a pressing concern. We will explore the role of external actors in influencing democratic processes and the consequences of such interference.

Finally, we will assess the long-term effects of electing leaders with socialist or leftist agendas. How do these agendas impact the economy, social policies, and the overall trajectory of a democracy?

In conclusion, this subchapter will delve into the challenges faced by democracies in maintaining stability during times of political polarization. By understanding the causes and consequences of polarization, scholars can gain insights into how to mitigate its negative effects and promote a healthier democratic system.

Navigating Divisions and Building Consensus

In the realm of democratic politics, divisions are inevitable. Diverse ideologies and competing interests often lead to a fractured society, making it difficult to achieve consensus. However, it is essential for the health of democracy that these divisions are navigated effectively, and attempts are made to build consensus among the different factions. This subchapter delves into the complexities of this process, exploring various strategies and their impact on democracy.

When democracy does not work, as evidenced by the examples of Palestinians electing Hamas, Nicaraguans electing Ortega, Chileans electing Allende, Americans electing Carter and Biden, it becomes crucial to understand the role of political parties in the democratic process. Political parties play a significant role in shaping the ideological landscape and mediating divisions within a society. By analyzing their influence, scholars can gain insights into how to bridge the gaps between different factions and foster consensus-building.

Moreover, the impact of socioeconomic factors on electoral outcomes cannot be ignored. Economic disparities, educational levels, and social mobility all influence voter behavior and contribute to divisions within society. Understanding these factors is key to developing effective strategies for building consensus.

The rise of populist leaders in democratic societies is another challenge that needs to be addressed. Populist leaders often thrive on divisions and exploit societal grievances for political gain. Assessing the consequences of electing leaders with controversial ideologies is essential to understanding the long-term implications for democracy.

This subchapter also explores the relationship between democracy and radical political movements. The success or failure of a democratic system in managing political transitions is crucial for maintaining stability. It examines how the efficacy of democratic systems is tested during times of political polarization and investigates the challenges faced by democracies in maintaining stability.

Additionally, the factors influencing voter behavior in democratic elections, such as media influence, campaign strategies, and foreign interference, are analyzed. Understanding these factors helps scholars assess the role of foreign interference in democratic elections and its impact on building consensus within a society.

Lastly, the long-term effects of electing leaders with socialist or leftist agendas are evaluated. By studying historical examples, scholars can gain insights into the challenges faced by democracies and the implications for consensus-building.

Overall, navigating divisions and building consensus is a critical aspect of maintaining a healthy democracy. This subchapter provides scholars with a comprehensive analysis of the strategies, challenges, and long-term consequences associated with this process. By exploring these topics, scholars can gain a deeper understanding of how to foster consensus and navigate divisions in diverse democratic societies.

Strengthening Democratic Institutions for Stability and Governance

In the modern political landscape, the strength and effectiveness of democratic institutions are crucial for maintaining stability and ensuring good governance. This subchapter will delve into the various factors that influence the stability of democratic systems and highlight the importance of strengthening democratic institutions.

When democracy does not work, it raises questions about the viability and resilience of democratic systems. This subchapter will examine specific case studies where controversial leaders were elected, such as Hamas in Palestine, Ortega in Nicaragua, Allende in Chile, and Carter and Biden in the United States. By analyzing these examples, scholars can gain insights into the consequences of electing leaders with controversial ideologies and the impact it has on democracy.

Political parties play a vital role in the democratic process. This subchapter will explore the significance of political parties in shaping the political landscape, influencing voter behavior, and safeguarding democratic values. It will also examine the challenges faced by political parties in maintaining their relevance and effectiveness in an ever-changing political climate.

Socioeconomic factors can significantly influence electoral outcomes. This subchapter will investigate how economic inequality, poverty, and unemployment can shape voter behavior and impact the democratic process. By understanding the relationship between socioeconomic factors and electoral outcomes, scholars can develop strategies to address these issues and promote more equitable democratic systems.

The rise of populist leaders in democratic societies has become a prominent global phenomenon. This subchapter will examine the factors that contribute to the emergence of populist leaders and the implications for democratic governance. It will analyze the appeal of populist rhetoric, the impact on democratic institutions, and the challenges faced in countering populist movements.

Additionally, this subchapter will assess the long-term effects of electing leaders with socialist or leftist agendas. By studying the experiences of countries that have elected such leaders, scholars can evaluate the success and challenges associated with implementing socialist policies within democratic systems.

Furthermore, it will explore the challenges faced by democracies in maintaining stability during times of political polarization. This subchapter will analyze the causes and consequences of political polarization and identify strategies to mitigate its negative effects on democratic institutions.

Overall, this subchapter will provide scholars with a comprehensive understanding of the various factors influencing the stability and governance of democratic systems. By examining real-world case studies and analyzing the impact of controversial ideologies on democracy, scholars can develop insights and strategies to strengthen democratic institutions and promote stable governance.